Bridgestone
B O O K S

Tsunamis

Thomas K. Adamson

Consultant:
Dr. Walter C. Dudley
Professor of Oceanography
University of Hawaii at Hilo
Chair, Scientific Advisory Council
Pacific Tsunami Museum

Capstone
press

Mankato, Minnesota

Bridgestone Books are published by Capstone Press,
151 Good Counsel Drive, P.O. Box 669, Mankato, Minnesota 56002.
www.capstonepress.com

Library of Congress Cataloging-in-Publication Data
Adamson, Thomas K., 1970–
    Tsunamis / by Thomas K. Adamson.
        p. cm.—(Bridgestone books)
    Includes bibliographical references and index.
    ISBN 0-7368-5248-4 (hardcover)
    1. Tsunamis—Juvenile literature. I. Title. II. Series.
GC221.5.A43 2006
551.46'37—dc22   2005001640

Summary: Explains how tsunamis form, how they move, the damage they cause, and how
    the 2004 tsunami affected South Asia and the world.

Editorial Credits
Chris Harbo, editor; Capstone Press Design Department, book design; Linda Clavel and
    Patrick D. Dentinger, illustrators; Deirdre Barton, photo researcher/photo editor

Photo Credits
Cover image: a tsunami wave rushing over a beach in Phuket, Thailand, on December 26, 2004, Getty
Images Inc./AFP/Joanne Davis

Title page image: the Forestry Department of Aceh in Indonesia using elephants to clear debris from the
2004 tsunami, VII/James Nachtwey

Corbis/Reuters/Beawiharta, 16; Thomas White, 20
Getty Images Inc./AFP/AFP, 6; AFP/Joanne Davis, 14; Paula Bronstein, 4
NOAA Corps/Commander Emily B. Christman, 18

Table of Contents

4

December 26, 2004

It began as a peaceful day on Thailand's west coast. Villagers fished in the ocean. Tourists relaxed on the beaches.

Suddenly, the ocean water retreated from the beach. Minutes later, a huge wall of water rushed back toward shore. Some people ran inland. Others climbed on top of roofs or held on to trees. Many people could not escape.

The wall of water was a tsunami that swept across the Indian Ocean. Its huge waves struck 12 countries in South Asia and Africa. It left at least 300,000 people dead or missing.

◄ Restaurants, shops, and houses lie in pieces after the 2004 tsunami struck Phi Phi Island, Thailand.

What Is a Tsunami?

A tsunami is a series of huge waves. In Japanese, tsunami means "harbor wave." Tsunamis hit coasts as fast-moving floods of water. The waves often destroy everything in their paths.

About five or six small tsunamis happen around the world each year. Most tsunamis happen in the Pacific Ocean. Tsunamis are rare in the world's other three oceans. But any large body of water can have a tsunami. In 1908, a tsunami in the Mediterranean Sea killed thousands of people in Italy.

◀ A huge tsunami wave rushes toward Malaysia's shore on December 26, 2004.

Earth's Plates

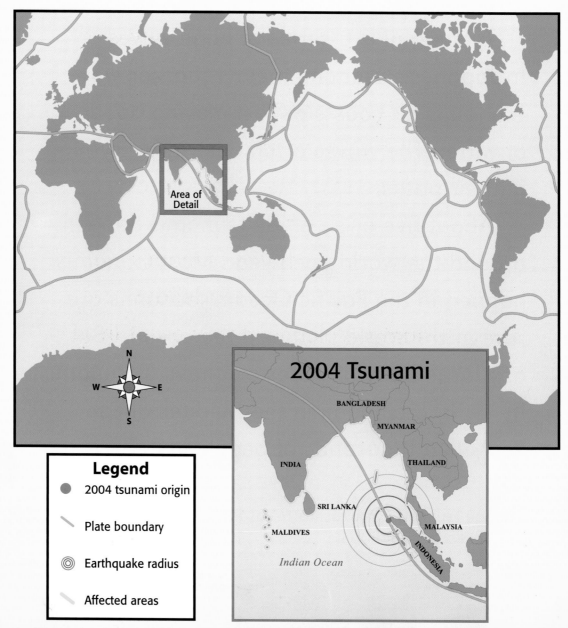

2004 Tsunami

BANGLADESH

MYANMAR

INDIA

THAILAND

SRI LANKA

MALAYSIA

MALDIVES

INDONESIA

Indian Ocean

Legend

● 2004 tsunami origin

╲ Plate boundary

◎ Earthquake radius

╲ Affected areas

How Tsunamis Begin

Earthquakes cause most tsunamis. An earthquake happens when the huge **plates** in the earth's surface slide against each other. A strong underwater earthquake causes a tsunami by forcing large amounts of water up and down.

Other events can cause tsunamis. Falling rocks and dirt from huge **landslides** can start tsunamis. Volcanoes that erupt in or near the ocean can also cause tsunamis. Very rarely, tsunamis are caused by large **meteorites** crashing into the ocean.

◀ Huge plates in the earth's surface fit together like a puzzle. The 2004 tsunami happened when two plates suddenly moved.

Tsunami Wave Creation

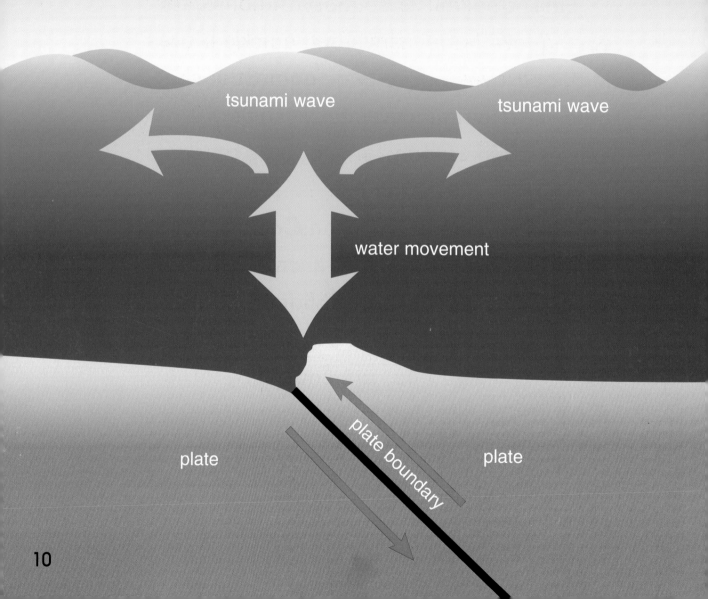

Making the Wave

Next time you're in the bathtub, sit still until the water is calm. Then quickly lift one leg up. Waves will splash against the sides of the tub. Tsunami waves begin the same way.

The 2004 tsunami was caused by the second largest earthquake in 100 years. Two plates under the Indian Ocean suddenly shifted. A 750-mile (1,200-kilometer) section of ocean floor moved about 65 feet (20 meters). The shifting plates caused a huge amount of water to move up and down. The moving water sent waves racing across the ocean.

◀ Deep in the ocean, a shift in the earth's plates can move enough water to cause a tsunami.

Tsunami Wave Movement

tsunami wave

How Tsunamis Move

In deep water, tsunami waves can reach speeds of 600 miles (970 kilometers) per hour. In 1960, a tsunami started near Chile in South America. It raced more than 10,000 miles (16,000 kilometers) across the Pacific Ocean. It hit Hawaii and Japan in less than 24 hours.

In the deep ocean, tsunami waves rise very little. Far from land, people on boats do not notice when a tsunami passes under them. As the tsunami reaches shore, the waves slow down and grow taller. The waves can grow to 100 feet (30 meters) high or more.

◀ Tsunami waves can move across the ocean as fast as a jet airplane. Near shore, the waves slow down and grow taller.

Reaching Shore

When a tsunami approaches, people on shore first notice that the ocean water often withdraws. Then they hear a roar like thunder. Minutes later, a wall of water rushes toward shore. The water looks like it is boiling. Unlike a regular wave, tsunami waves come ashore as a rush of churning water.

The waves move in a series called a wave train. Waves in the train can be an hour apart. After the first wave hits, people might think the danger has passed. Then another, more powerful wave crashes ashore.

◄ Water pours over the beach and through a restaurant in Phuket, Thailand, during the 2004 tsunami.

Damage

Tsunamis can destroy everything along a coastline. Boats, cars, and buildings near the shore are instantly smashed by the wall of water. The waves have enough force to knock over trains. The 2004 tsunami in South Asia pushed water more than 5 miles (8 kilometers) inland in some places.

Tsunami waves aren't done causing damage when they roll ashore. Soon, the water heads back to the ocean, washing **debris** and people out to sea.

◄ Banda Aceh, Indonesia, looked like a junkyard after the 2004 tsunami. Cars and broken buildings were pushed into huge piles.

Warning Systems

Warning systems help scientists detect earthquakes and tsunami waves. Some equipment sits on the ocean floor. It measures changes in **water pressure** when a tsunami wave passes over it. This information is sent to a **buoy** on the surface. Scientists gather the information and issue warnings.

In 2004, the Indian Ocean didn't have these warning systems. In addition, many people in the tsunami's path didn't have TVs, phones, or e-mail. Even if warnings had been sent, they may not have reached many people.

◄ Scientists put a tsunami buoy into the ocean. The buoy is part of a tsunami warning system in the Pacific Ocean.

After the 2004 Tsunami

The 2004 tsunami in the Indian Ocean killed thousands of people. Millions of survivors lost their homes. People were left without clean water to drink or food to eat.

Soon after the disaster, the world helped. Many countries flew in medicine, food, and clean water. **Relief organizations** collected money and supplies to help people who had lost their families and homes.

Huge tsunamis don't happen very often. Scientists are studying the 2004 tsunami to protect people from tsunamis in the future.

◀ A Buddhist monk gives food to survivors of the 2004 tsunami in Sri Lanka.

Glossary

buoy (BOO-ee)—a floating marker in the ocean

debris (duh-BREE)—the remains of something that has
been destroyed

earthquake (URTH-kwayk)—a sudden, violent shaking of the
ground caused by shifting plates in the earth's surface

landslide (LAND-slide)—a large mass of earth and rocks that
suddenly slides down a mountain or hill

meteorite (MEE-tee-ur-rite)—a piece of rock from space that
strikes a planet or a moon

plate (PLAYT)—a large sheet of rock that is a piece of the
earth's crust

relief organization (ri-LEEF or-guh-nuh-ZAY-shuhn)—a group
that gives money, food, supplies, and other help to people
in need

water pressure (WAH-tur PRESH-ur)—the force of water
pressing on something

Read More

Bonar, Samantha. *Tsunamis.* Natural Disasters. Mankato, Minn.: Capstone Press, 2002.

Spilsbury, Louise, and Richard Spilsbury. *Sweeping Tsunamis.* Awesome Forces of Nature. Chicago: Heinemann, 2003.

Internet Sites

FactHound offers a safe, fun way to find Internet sites related to this book. All of the sites on FactHound have been researched by our staff.

Here's how:
1. Visit *www.facthound.com*
2. Type in this special code **0736852484** for age-appropriate sites. Or enter a search word related to this book for a more general search.
3. Click on the **Fetch It** button.

FactHound will fetch the best sites for you!

Index